UPS & DOWNS

How to Beat the Blues and Teen Depression

Written by Susan Klebanoff, Ph.D.
and Ellen Luborsky, Ph.D.

Illustrated by Andy Cooke

PSS!
PRICE STERN SLOAN

Authors' Note: The quotes and case examples in this book come from our clinical experience, but all names and identifying details have been changed to protect our patients' privacy. The quotations exemplify the problems discussed, but are not verbatim statements of any individual.

Copyright © 1999 by Susan Klebanoff and Ellen Luborsky. Illustrations copyright © 1999 by Andy Cooke. All rights reserved. Published by Price Stern Sloan, Inc., a member of Penguin Putnam Books for Young Readers, New York. Printed in the United States of America. Published simultaneously in Canada. No part of this publication may be reproduced, stored in a retrieval system, or transmitted, in any form or by any means, electronic, mechanical, photocopying, recording or otherwise, without the prior written permission of the publisher.

Library of Congress Cataloging-in-Publication Data
Klebanoff, Susan.
    Ups & downs : how to beat the blues and teen depression / written by Susan Klebanoff and Ellen Luborsky.
        p.   cm — (Plugged in)
    Summary: Examines the nature, causes, and effects of depression, where to turn for help, and ways to cope with it.
    1. Depression in adolescence—Juvenile literature. [1. Depression, Mental.] I. Luborsky, Ellen. II. Title. III. Title: Ups and downs. IV. Series.
    RF506.D4K58   1998
    616.85'27—dc21   98-46802
                                                            CIP
    ISBN 0-8431-7450-1 (pb)   A B C D E F G H I J   AC
    ISBN 0-8431-7460-9 (GB)   A B C D E F G H I J

Plugged in is a trademark of Price Stern Sloan, Inc.
PSS! is a registered trademark of Price Stern Sloan, Inc.

Contents

Introduction

Do you ever feel like you don't want to get out of bed? Like what's the point, everything in your life is going wrong, and nobody cares? Your family doesn't understand you, your friends don't want to hear it, your teachers keep piling on the work and you just can't take it anymore. You're tired of people telling you to cheer up and get over it. Life sucks. It really sucks.

You may just be in a bad mood...or is it something more?

Bad moods happen to everyone. No one goes through life without feeling down, sad, or out of it at least once in a while. And as a teenager, you're going through a time in your life when a lot of changes are taking place—changes that affect your mind and body, and your moods.

This book is *not* about how never to be in a bad mood again. Nobody can do that. But it is about how to stop a bad mood from keeping you down—or, if it is keeping you down, how to do something about it.

1

Two Stories

Kim

It was the worst week ever. Mme. Gilbert handed back the French test, and can you believe it? I got an F! Right there, I almost passed out. I had to sit through the rest of the class feeling awful. All I could think was, if I tell my mom, she'll freak! Probably I'll be grounded for a week or a month or, like, my life.

So, okay. At first I wanted to talk to Lena about it. I mean, should I tell my parents? But when I walked into the cafeteria I didn't see Lena anywhere. Only guess what I did see? Suzanne talking to Damion, and laughing! And she knew I liked him first. So I left. Goodbye, cafeteria. Forget lunch. Still, I had to sit through four more classes before I could get out of school.

Finally, I got home. But everyone was annoying me, especially at dinner.

They kept on talking when all I wanted was peace and quiet. My mom asked me, "Is something bothering you?" But I didn't dare tell her.

Then, get this, nobody called that night. I mean the phone was dead. Lena didn't call. Suzanne didn't call. And I thought maybe Damion would call me, but he didn't either. So I tried to do my homework, but I couldn't keep my mind on it. It was like nobody cared. I mean, they didn't call.

I turned on the TV and watched whatever came on. It was better than thinking about that stupid test. Then I just went to bed, but I couldn't sleep. Couldn't get comfortable. Even the rain was too noisy.

The rest of the week was a waste. All my classes ran together into one big whatever. I still took notes, but every single teacher was boring.

Friends were nowhere. I didn't go near the cafeteria because I couldn't deal with the scene there, I mean, all those happy people, and who knows what was happening with Suzanne and Damion. Lucky I had Doritos in my locker, so I didn't starve.

Finally, on Friday, Lena called. She asked me, "Where have you been all week?" It turned out she had been looking for me and I didn't even know it.

I asked her how come she didn't call me—and she said she did. My stupid little sister never gave me the messages! Can you believe that?

Then Lena wanted to know, "Are you okay? What's going on?"

So I told her about the whole week—Damion, the French test, everything. She said Damion doesn't even like Suzanne, he told her. Okay. But the French test, I said, that's really bad. And she said she got an F too, in algebra once. That totally amazed me, because Lena's one of those straight-A students.

"Do you think I should tell my parents?" I asked her. But even before she answered, I was feeling a lot better. And I could just tell she didn't think it was all so terrible. She said, "Tell if you want—or you can always go to the teacher and see if she'll let you take a re-test or do extra credit or something."

Lena started me thinking. I was so stressed out, I kind of forgot—I can do something about this.

Now let's go to the other side of Mme. Gilbert's French class, over by the window. Kim didn't know it, but someone else got an F on the test, too.

Zack

Who needs this? What's the point of studying if you're going to get a grade like that?

I crumpled up my paper and shoved it in my pocket. This class sucks. This school sucks! I mean, this whole year has been a waste.

Last year was way different. I was, like, perfect on the soccer

5

field—me and Brian both. That's how we got to be co-captains. You should have seen us pass. Our timing was awesome. It was like we couldn't lose. Then Brian had to move to California. His dad got a job out there. Nothing I could do about that. But soccer without Brian, it just wasn't the same game.

Home wasn't the same either. There was nothing worth doing. It used to be I didn't need to have something to do. I could just hang out with my dog Casey. She could pass a ball like a person! I got her for my thirteenth birthday. Then my brother got allergic. Sneezing and wheezing all the time. So the doctor said we had to get rid of her. Nothing I could do about that, either.

After that I just felt like, what's the point of trying? At school. Even at soccer. I told the coach I had too much work to do to stay on the team. But really, it wasn't that. Really, I'd been playing lousy and I didn't want to let the team down. All I needed was for them to be mad at me.

The guys kept asking me how come I wasn't playing ball anymore. I didn't know what to say, so I kind of just stayed away from them. So then I had nobody to hang with.

School got bad. I couldn't concentrate in class—it took way too much energy—so I started bombing on everything. I couldn't deal with homework either. When I got home from school, I just went right to sleep. My teachers sent home warning notes for my parents. But that was easy. I just threw them away.

This went on for a while. I mean months. It was like I was living in this gray world where nothing was fun and nothing could make it better. I even thought, what's the point of going on? I mean, no one would notice if I wasn't around and probably they wouldn't care.

It got hard to sleep at night since I slept all afternoon, so I would stay up and watch TV. Then I'd go to school exhausted, come home, and fall into bed all over again.

I pretty much stopped eating meals—it was just too much trouble. Anyway, I'd kind of lost my appetite. So I'd stay up in my room. My parents didn't make me come down for dinner. They figured it was just a phase I was going through.

They didn't notice anything was wrong till my next report card came.

Then my dad went ballistic. I failed two subjects, French and bio, and did pretty awful in everything else. The report card was full of comments about my attitude problem, too.

"What's the matter with you?!" he yelled. I mean, I'd always been this good student. "And what are you planning to do about this?" he wanted to know.

I didn't know what was wrong. And I sure didn't know what to do about it.

The week starts the same way for Kim and Zack. They both fail the same French test. They both get upset about it, and neither one of them knows what to do. They both avoid everyone and feel discouraged about school.

But what's different? Kim's funk lasts only a week. Her everyday life isn't disrupted by her mood for long. She skips lunch a few times, but she doesn't lose her appetite. She has no trouble sleeping, except for that first night. That can happen to anybody.

Kim gets in a mood where everything bothers her. But it doesn't get so bad that she withdraws from everything— at least not for long. It doesn't get so bad that she can't put the brakes on it, with a little help from her best friend.

The most important thing is that Kim's mood lifts pretty quickly. It helps to talk to Lena about her grade. That makes her feel less alone and less like there's something wrong with her. It's just one grade! She feels better when she realizes there's something she can do about it, too.

But what about Zack? Zack is stuck in a bad mood that keeps getting worse. All the things that used to make him feel good, like hanging out with his friends and playing ball, don't work anymore. Nothing makes him feel better. While Kim gets back into her life pretty quickly, Zack just can't.

At school, he really can't concentrate, so it's impossible to keep up with his work. Each day puts him farther behind, so he ends up feeling hopeless about ever catching up. He loses his energy and appetite, too. He has trouble sleeping, so he's always tired during the day. Everything feels out of his control.

Zack doesn't understand what's going on, but he does know he's way too embarrassed to talk to anyone about it. He doesn't want people to think there is something wrong with him. He wants to keep up his image—as the guy who has it all together.

By the time Zack's parents find out there's a problem (by seeing his report card), he's already been in trouble for months. He's slipped into a depression. And no one has realized it—not even Zack.

Depression is not the same as sadness. In conversation, people often say "depressed" when they actually mean "sad." The difference is that sadness is a perfectly normal reaction to something bad that happens, like a friend moving away or someone you love dying. Or you might just wake up feeling sad or crummy one day for no apparent reason at all. And while normal sadness goes away after a short period of time—a few days or, at most, a few weeks—depression lasts and lasts and can seep into other areas of your life.

Changes

How come nobody realized Zack was having a such a serious problem? How come even he didn't know he was depressed? The teen years are a time of huge changes—in the way you look, feel, and act. People expect teens to change, so they often overlook signs of serious problems like Zack's.

What are the normal changes that every teenager goes through? Becoming a teenager means morphing out of that little kid body into someone who looks grown up. The changes in your body are caused by hormones that started building in your body when you were eight or nine. By the time you become a teenager, those hormones are in the process of turning you into a man or a woman—about the biggest biological change in your life!

The same hormones that are turning you into an adult can also make you more moody. Maybe you're happy one minute, and then get plunged into a bad mood when something goes wrong (look at Kim!). Even little things can set you off before you even know what's happening—it's kind of like trying to ride a horse that has a mind of its own.

I was talking to this girl I liked, and my mom asked me to get off the phone. I did it, but then I yelled, "Can't you ever leave me alone? Just get out of my life!"

Ian, 13

So I'm late for a party and I can't find my favorite jeans anywhere! Suddenly, I just burst into tears!

Kate, 14

This is pretty typical of what just about everyone goes through. But sometimes, for a mix of reasons, moods can get out of hand. They can turn into serious problems, like they did for Zack. How can you tell if what you're feeling is something more? How can you tell if it's depression? Here's what you need to look for.

SIGNS OF DEPRESSION

1. You're in a sad or irritable mood nearly every day.

2. You've lost interest in the things you usually like to do. Nothing cheers you up or gives you pleasure anymore.

3. Your appetite changes dramatically. Maybe you eat nonstop after school, or you skip lots of meals because you just don't feel hungry.

4. Your sleep pattern changes. You might not be able to sleep at night, or you might want to sleep all the time (more than ten hours a night).

5. You are agitated, or else very slowed down, almost every day.

6. You feel tired and have no energy almost all the time.

7. You feel worthless and guilty nearly every day. (This means feeling guilty over things that are not even your fault.)

8. You have a lot of trouble concentrating or making decisions.

9. You have thoughts or plans about suicide. *This sign is important!* See the box on page 14 for what to do about it.

It's entirely possible that you might have one of these feelings now and then. Join the club! That's not unusual. Or maybe you've had one of the symptoms for a couple of days—like, say you're feeling bored, sad, or irritable, but you're not having trouble eating or sleeping...or something really bad just happened and you're still upset over it, even though you keep going on with the things you're supposed to. That may not be anything to worry about either.

What isn't okay is having several of these symptoms for days and days and days. If you have one of the first two symptoms and four of the others on this list for at least two weeks, you may have something called a *clinical depression*—a serious illness that affects not only your mood but your mind and body, too—and, just like Zack, you need to find help to get you out of it.

Even if you have just one of the symptoms on this list, if you have it every day for a long time and nothing seems to make it go away, that's a sign that you may have a mild form of depression. This, too, needs your attention so it doesn't turn into something worse.

Are the symptoms on this list the only signs of depression? No. Not all serious mood problems show up this way, especially when you are a teenager. Drinking, doing drugs, and getting into trouble at school are just some of the other ways teens can act out what's really a deeper emotional problem like depression. Chapter 3 will tell you about the kinds of depression that don't look like depression.

No matter how it shows up, depression is a problem for lots of teens. In fact, statistics say that as many as one in five adolescents will go through a serious depression. But what some of them don't know is that depression is very curable. People with depression can and do get better, and turn their lives around.

For teenage moods and even for mild depression, there are lots of things you can do all by yourself to pull out of it. For clinical depression, you'll want to get the right professional help. That's not as hard as you may think.

Getting depressed does not mean you are weird or crazy or doomed. And it's definitely not your fault! But it does mean you need to pay special attention to yourself—your moods, your thoughts, your feelings, and your actions. Figuring out if you are depressed and finding out how and why you feel the way you do are the first steps to knowing what to do about it. This book will show you how.

Have You Ever Thought About Suicide?

If you *ever* find yourself thinking you don't want to wake up to another day or that you'd be better off dead, this is serious! If you have a plan to hurt yourself—no matter how far-fetched—don't wait: Turn to Chapter 5, "How Other People Can Help." No matter how hopeless you're feeling, you can change things.

What If It's a Friend?

If a friend tells you he or she is thinking about suicide, the same guidelines apply. You really can't know how serious the situation is. It is always safer to take suicidal talk seriously rather than shrug it off.

Other warning signs of suicide include giving away precious personal belongings and dwelling on the subject of death. Kids who talk a lot about their own funerals—even as a joke—can also be in real distress.

If you promised not to tell about a friend's suicidal thoughts, this is one promise you can't afford to keep. Your friend may be mad at you, but telling a responsible adult is the only way to get him or her the help that's needed.

Question:

How can you tell the difference between someone only saying he's going to kill himself and someone who really will?

Answer:

You can't! It's better to be safe than sorry.

2

Why Me? Why Now?

How come some people get depressed and other people don't? Kim and Zack both failed the same French test. How come Zack went into a depression, while Kim just got stressed out for a week?

It's a good question, so good that researchers have been trying to solve it for a long time. The basic answer is that everybody's different. We all have different ways our bodies react, different ways in which we respond to stress, and different life experiences.

People are vulnerable in different ways, too. When some people get sick, they get sore throats. Other people more often end up with stomachaches. Some people never seem to get sick at all. These differences don't mean one kind of person is better than another. It's just the way they are. The same is true of depression.

Can you tell if a person is especially vulnerable to depression? Sometimes. For one thing, depression can run in a family, just the way allergies can. But if someone in your family has been seriously depressed, that does *not* mean you are fated to be too. It does mean that it will help you to learn more about dealing with your feelings, so you can do your best to stay healthy.

Other things can make you vulnerable too. Certain kinds of experiences can put you more at risk for depression. So can the way you handle stress.

Trauma

"It was totally traumatic!" Nikki was talking about how all the bathing suits she tried on made her look fat. It wasn't really traumatic—but that's how people use the word in conversation.

A trauma is actually a devastating event: a fire, a car crash, a shooting, a rape. A trauma shocks you to the core, so that nothing feels okay afterwards. You can get frightened by anything that reminds you of what happened. Your mind can keep on replaying the trauma in flashbacks and nightmares.

It's the kind of experience that can lead to depression. Anyone who has been through a trauma needs time to recover. Most people also need professional help to put it behind them. You can get help through Victim's Services or by finding a therapist who works with trauma. See the back of this book for sources of help.

Let's take a look at Zack to see how his experiences and

his personal style affected him. Even before Zack failed the French test, things had happened that were getting him down. It was like the logs were already stacked in the fireplace, when along came the match—that F!

Zack had gone through two losses in the last year: His best friend moved to California, and his family had to give away his dog. Zack had counted on his friend Brian—in soccer, in school, in his life—much more than he realized. When he lost Brian, he lost his motivation for the things they had done together. Zack's dog used to keep him company at home. He felt lonely and lost without her.

Zack didn't know how to cope with his feelings—he was too cool to admit that he was hurting. Hiding his feelings was no problem when everything was going well, but it was hard on him when nothing was going right. It was part of Zack's personality to pull away from people when he felt stressed. So the worse he felt, the more he withdrew. That made him even more vulnerable to depression, since other people can help when you are having a hard time.

Another part of Zack's personality got him in trouble: He was a perfectionist. He thought he had to be perfect on the ballfield and in school, too. For Zack, getting an F meant he was a failure. Not playing his best at soccer meant he shouldn't play, period. His self-esteem was all caught up in being perfect, so when things went wrong, he couldn't feel okay as a person.

All of Zack's problems snowballed. The different problems and feelings Zack was having built up and up, until they turned into something too big for him to deal with—depres-

sion. None of this was Zack's fault. He was trying to do his best. He just didn't know about the solutions there are for his kinds of problems.

What about Kim? When she got stressed out, how come it didn't turn into depression? Kim didn't withdraw completely. She was able to talk about what was bothering her. She could hear her friend Lena when she tried to help. Also, Kim had no losses to deal with, and she was not a perfectionist. She got upset but she climbed out of it before it turned into something more.

Triggers

So, how do you keep yourself from falling into a real depression? One way is to sharpen your awareness of your feelings.

Depression doesn't come out of nowhere, even though it

can seem that way. Something always happens to make you start feeling depressed. You might not even notice, but it's there. Psychologists call this a *trigger*. For Zack, the trigger was the F, but it could be anything.

When ninth grade started, I had lots of friends. I was even getting good grades. Then I don't know what happened. I just didn't feel like trying anymore. I got behind at school, and everyone got on my nerves. Then get this. My friends stopped calling.

Jenny, 15

What happened? What Jenny forgot to say was that at the beginning of ninth grade, the boy she had liked for a whole year asked out her best friend. Jenny didn't realize it then ("no biggie"), but she felt rejected. She stopped talking to people, and she stopped putting in an effort at school. She lost interest without really noticing what was happening to her. The rejection was Jenny's trigger.

Somebody else might have shrugged off what happened. It really got to Jenny because she was especially sensitive to feeling rejected. Of course, another person might get depressed over an experience that wouldn't bother Jenny at all. People have different sensitivities. If you can identify yours, you can be more aware of the kind of experiences that are especially hard for you.

There are a few very common triggers. Try this quiz and see what sets you off.

TRIGGER QUIZ

Rate these situations from 1 to 5.
1 = doesn't bother you   5 = terrible

1. Everyone but you passed the math test.

2. Your parents are talking about divorce.

3. Your oldest friend doesn't invite you to her party.

4. Kids at school tease you about what you're wearing.

5. Your parents are having a loud fight.

6. Your boyfriend/girlfriend wants to date other people.

7. You lose the tennis tournament because of an unfair call.

8. Your pet dies.

9. Your teacher yells at you.

10. Your mother keeps saying she's busy when you try to talk to her.

11. You apply for a great summer job and get turned down.

12. Someone is spreading a mean rumor about you.

13. A friend asks other kids to her beach house, but not you.

14. Your grandmother is critically ill.

15. Everyone at school has better clothes than you.

16. You change schools and miss your old friends.

17. Your dad gets really furious when you don't clear your place at the dinner table.

18. Your pants rip at a party, and there's no way for you to get home to change.

19. You're a total spaz at team sports.

20. Your best friend moves across the country.

SCORING

The triggers on this quiz fall into four general categories: loss, rejection, anger, and self-esteem setbacks. Look at the following list, write down the number you gave each question, and then add up the score you got for each category.

	Questions/Rating										Total
Loss:	2		8		14		16		20		
Rejection:	3		6		10		11		13		
Anger:	5		7		9		12		17		
Self-Esteem Setbacks:	1		4		15		18		19		

The category with the highest score is your most sensitive trigger. But take a look at the scores you get on the other categories, too. Any number greater than fifteen means you are sensitive in this area.

What's the point? Knowing your sensitivities—or triggers—will help you predict your reactions better and help you catch yourself before you get into emotional difficulty. Here are some suggestions on how to cope with these four key triggers.

Loss

Of all the triggers that can set off depression, loss is typically the most powerful one. Losses may be small or huge—they still affect you. Losing people that you are close to is usually the most painful loss of all. But losses of important places, pets, or even treasured things can be troubling.

The loss of a close family member always has a huge impact, no matter how well everyone seems to be coping.

After my grandma died, my priest suggested me and my parents go to a bereavement counselor. At first I didn't get why. My dad didn't even get along with her that great. But it helped to have a place to talk about things where no one was afraid to cry and stuff.
Alan, 12

The most common mistakes kids make in dealing with this kind of loss are (1) not talking about it in the first place ("She's gone. Talking about it can't fix what happened"), and (2) not wanting to upset parents who are already overwhelmed by the same loss. But talking about feelings gives you and your parents the chance to mourn and move forward. Mourning means letting yourself feel the sad feelings, and holding onto the good memories. Even with smaller losses, you need to express your feelings.

Rejection

What does it mean to be sensitive to rejection? It means that when anything happens that could make you feel the slightest bit rejected, you start to withdraw and feel bad about yourself. Remember Jenny? She started on a negative slide when the boy she liked asked out her best friend. But at first she didn't realize what was happening. Only by rereading her diary, which she'd kept ever since her eleventh birthday, did she figure out when she started to feel bad and why. That helped her gain perspective. The rejection felt bad, sure, but when she really thought about it, it was not worth getting sick over. Besides, the guy turned out to be a real dork!

When rejection happens, it's easy to take it to heart and think you're not worth anything. But people can learn to resist this kind of negative thinking.

Take a look at Chapter 4 to find out how.

Anger

For most people, anger is one of the most difficult feelings to deal with. People tend to think of anger as a bad thing, something to be avoided at all costs, even though it can be a perfectly normal, healthy reaction.

How can anger lead to depression? Anger directed at you can make you feel wounded and ashamed. If you have a problem getting angry, even when you have a good reason, you may turn your anger inward, at yourself.

Some people have trouble with any kind of anger. They hate feeling angry and they can't stand having someone angry at them. If you scored high on questions 5, 7, 9, 12, or 17, you may fall into this group.

If you scored high on questions 7 and 12, you may have

trouble handling your own anger. Maybe you have trouble showing anger, or maybe getting angry is all too easy. There are strategies for handling both problems.

I used to get into all these fights at hockey and I didn't like how much time I was spending in the penalty box. The coach worked with me on how to slow things down when I was about to lose my temper. A few deep breaths and a short time-out helped clear my head and then I'd go out on the ice again.

Joey, 14

My friend Carol is late for everything and I'm always waiting for her. I was afraid to get angry because I thought it would spoil our friendship. But one day—after waiting forty-five minutes in the rain— I had to say something. I told her it made me mad that I was always waiting. Carol apologized and we stayed friends. She's still late, but not as late, and anyway, it doesn't bother me the same way because I know I can call her on it.

Jane, 13

If you scored high on questions 5, 9, or 17, you may be having trouble handling other people's anger. That's something you can't always avoid. For instance, maybe you have to stand up for yourself with that unfair teacher. Or you have to learn to put up with your sister's temper tantrums because you can't just always give in. It can take practice to cope with this tricky emotion.

Self-Esteem Setbacks

If you have a high score in this category, you need to work on improving your self-esteem. Having shaky self-esteem is like building a house without a foundation. If you don't feel good about yourself, it's way too easy for a negative experience to tip the balance and leave you feeling crushed.

When you're a teenager, it's impossible to feel good about yourself all the time. There's too much personal change and social pressure. And the challenges to your self-esteem can seem endless. One day you're dissed for having the wrong clothes, another day for hanging out with the wrong person. But if you don't feel good about yourself most of the time, there are some things you can do about it. Check out the self-esteem secrets in Chapter 4.

Stress

Everybody has stress in their lives—like when there's that test coming up, or when you have a fight with your best friend. But sometimes a stressful situation doesn't go away. And that can make you more vulnerable to depression. Often you can't do much about the situation itself, but you can learn how to help yourself cope with the stress it causes.

Family Stress

Who doesn't have family stress? We all do. All families

have times when they're under pressure or they're not communicating so well. But when family stress is serious and ongoing, it changes your home life and affects how you feel about yourself. Some family stresses are obvious—like a parents' divorce or separation, financial problems, drug or alcohol problems, unemployment, or a serious illness.

Abuse

My dad is vice president of his company and a deacon in the church. Everybody says hello to him like they respect him so much. I wish I did. They don't know what he used to be like at home. Anytime he got drunk, he'd go off on me. I don't mean just yell a little. He'd throw things and curse at me something awful. I'd just freeze till it was over. I couldn't tell anybody. I was too ashamed. This was my father! It wasn't until my uncle got him to go to AA that he changed. Then I had to go to teen meetings to learn it wasn't all my fault.

Jon, 14

Kids who are abused often feel that they are to blame. But abuse is never the kid's fault. Abuse happens when someone else's behavior is out of control and is harming other people. That goes for physical abuse, sexual abuse, and even verbal abuse.

If anyone abuses you, get help to make it stop. Tell a responsible adult—a family member, a school counselor, or someone at your religious school. Or call the abuse hotline at 1-800-422-4453. You have a right to grow up safe.

Others are less obvious—like families that have a lot of conflict, overly critical families, and even families that are extremely protective.

There are a few good rules to follow for dealing with stress in the family.

1. Remember it's not your fault.
2. Understand that you can't take responsibility for fixing a family problem.
3. Keep your own life on track.
4. Find a safe haven where there are nice, concerned people: a friend or relative's house, an after-school activity, a church or synagogue, or even a part-time job.
5. Reach out to others.

Illness

I got mono, a really bad case. I had to stay out of school for months. I felt really strange when I finally went back.

Vanessa, 13

If you're physically ill and out of school for an extended period of time, one way to keep from getting down or even falling into a depression is to stay in touch with your friends. Try to have them visit. If visiting is out of the question, use E-mail or the phone. The more in touch you stay, the better off you'll feel and the easier it will be for you to reenter your "healthy" world. Remember, even when you're recovering, illness can still zap your energy and interfere with your normal activities.

If you're suffering from an unusual or very serious illness, try to find a way to contact other kids with similar problems. Your doctor may be able to hook you up with a local support group.

Also, make sure you talk to your doctor about how you feel emotionally as well as physically. Certain medical conditions—and medicines—can make you feel depressed. Medication can sometimes be changed to make you feel better. A healthy emotional state is an important weapon in the fight against physical illness.

Differences

During adolescence, conformity rules. Anything that makes you feel different from everybody else can create stress. You can get teased, harassed, or left out for differences. Or other kids can be okay about it, but knowing you're different can make you feel left out and alone inside.

Maybe your race, your religion, or your ethnic group puts you in a minority in your community.

I went to an all-white school—all white except for me and about two other kids. I knew I was getting a good education, but I felt like this random person. So my dad got together a group of kids like me—black kids in mostly white private schools—and we had a meeting every month to talk about what we were going through. It helped!

Mohammed, 13

Like Mohammed, you can try looking for friends and groups that will make you feel less isolated.

Differences in sexual development can be a big issue during the teen years. Everyone's self-conscious about the changes they are going through. If you happen to develop more quickly or more slowly than the majority, you can get teased and be made to feel even more self-conscious.

It was like all of a sudden I needed a bra. I mean a size C bra. And then guys were staring straight at my chest all the time. It was so bad! I started wearing a baggy sweatshirt, even in the summer. Later on, the other girls caught up with me, more or less, and it wasn't such a big deal anymore. I wish I could have known in seventh grade that was going to happen.

Debbie, 15

There can be other issues around sex, too. For instance, kids sometimes question their sexual orientation during high school. For some, this questioning is the first step to coming to terms with their homosexuality. For others it is part of growing up and getting comfortable with sexual feelings.

In high school I felt weird, different—but I didn't know why. Looking back, I realized it was because I was gay and I hadn't figured that out.

Mike, 19

All my friends were talking guys, guys, guys...isn't this one cute...isn't that one amazing...and I didn't feel attracted to guys at all, so I wondered if maybe I was gay. Then I met Josh and it was settled. I was definitely attracted to him.

Lauren, 14

Learning differences can also make kids feel cut off from their peers. If this is your situation, try to remember that learning differences don't make you "less smart" and build on your strengths.

School was hard for me because I saw some letters backward. Teachers were always telling me to slow down and take my time. But when I got out on the ski slopes, boy, could I go. It was so cool: I was a natural.

Zack, 14

Even your special interests or hobbies can make you feel different.

I was crazy about chess since fifth grade. But when I got to middle school that made me a nerd. It took forever for me to get the nerve to join the Chess Club, but after I did I liked it so much I didn't care what anyone thought.

Tony, 13

If people treat you as if there's something wrong because you are different from them in some way, don't take it to heart. That's a setup for getting depressed. Remember, we're all different in one way or another. If we were exactly the same, the world would be a boring place.

3

When Depression Doesn't Look Like Depression

Most people think of depression as a feeling of unhappiness that overwhelms your life. They're not wrong; clinical depression can do just that. But depression can show up in many other ways, too. Sometimes behavior that people shrug off as typical adolescent rebellion and moodiness can actually be signs of deeper problems. Teens especially can show their depression in ways that don't look like depression at all.

Your Body Speaks

Sometimes pains in your body are really messages about how you feel. It can be easier for some people to talk about their bodies hurting than to talk about hurt feelings. This doesn't mean the physical pain isn't real, but that it has an emotional source.

Every single day before school, I woke up with a stomachache. I kept being late because I felt so sick. After a month or so, my dad took me to the doctor to see what was wrong. The doctor did these gross tests, and then he said I was okay. Nothing was wrong! So I asked him what I could do to make my stomach stop hurting. He suggested I go talk to a therapist; maybe it was caused by my feelings. I thought that was pretty lame, but my dad said to give it a try.

He took me to a psychiatrist and I found out pretty quick that the doctor was right. My stomach stopped hurting after I talked about what was going on. See, my mom had started commuting out of town for a new job and just coming home on weekends. I hadn't told anybody about it because I was afraid they would think I was a baby for missing my mother.

After I figured out what the problem was, I still missed her, but I didn't need my stomach to talk for me. And when my dad explained that to my mom, she started calling me every morning.

Mark, 13

Stomachaches, headaches, or even other pains can sometimes have more to do with your feelings than you'd think.

If you have constant pains, you need to go to the doctor to see if there is a medical problem, just like Mark did. If there isn't, then think about what's been happening in your life lately.

Eating Disorders

Most teenagers try crazy diets or totally pig out once in a while. But about one in five girls go much farther. They develop an eating disorder—a serious illness that has to do with your body image and how you use (or abuse) food in your life.

Depression typically goes along with an eating disorder. Focusing on food can be a way of trying to forget unhappy feelings. But if you're kind of depressed to start with, the eating disorder will make you feel worse. Most people don't know it, but eating disorders are also addictive, like drugs and alcohol. After you get hooked, it's very hard to stop. That's why it's good to work out these problems as soon as you can.

Bingeing

Every day when I came home from school, I'd head straight for the refrigerator. I'd tell myself I'm not going to do it, but it would happen anyway. I'd start eating and I just couldn't stop.

Nicole, 13

For some people, a box of Oreo's is more available than a friend or parent. Food can fill the emptiness, and comfort you when you're down. But guess what? It doesn't work for long. After bingeing, people usually feel worse, not better.

Nicole started overeating in the seventh grade. The apartment was empty when she got home from school. Her parents had split up; her mom had gotten a job; her older sister had gone off to college. Nicole felt the urge to eat as soon as she saw that empty place.

By Christmas vacation, Nicole had gained fifteen pounds. Her mom got worried and called Overeaters Anonymous for help. They referred Nicole to a specialist in eating disorders who worked with her to break her overeating habit, get in touch with her feelings, and get her life back on track. Her mom also met with a counselor so she could learn how to be helpful to Nicole. She started calling each day when Nicole got home from school, and leaving healthy snacks in the fridge. And she arranged for Nicole to go home with a friend after school two days a week. All that made Nicole feel less lonely and more comfortable taking care of herself. She stopped turning to food to feel better.

Bulimia

My friend Sally told me she knew how to eat whatever you want and still not gain weight. First, she'd pig out—on cookies, ice cream, whatever—then she'd force herself to throw up. It sounded so gross.

I was feeling sort of fat one day and I thought of trying what Sally did. But Sally ended up passing out in school that exact same day. She had to go to the hospital! After Sally got sick, the school nurse talked to us about the dangers of throwing up a lot—you can get heart problems, rot your teeth, and mess up your stomach so you are throwing up when you don't want to! I'm glad I never tried it.

Allison, 14

Can you relate to Sally's story? Lots of people are tempted to binge and throw up. But this is a trap. What really happens is that you get caught in an addictive cycle with behavior you can't control. For help with bulimia, look at the listings on eating disorders at the back of this book.

Anorexia

It started with a diet. After the first five pounds I wanted to lose five more and then five more. Before long, all I could think about was losing more weight. I was sort of in my own little world. I ignored my hunger pains. After a while, I stopped feeling hungry, but I started having headaches, getting dizzy, and being freezing cold, even when it was hot. One day this guy Gary said, "You look like a skeleton, girl." I didn't know what he was talking about. But then I went shopping with my mom for summer clothes and she got a good look at me.

"This has gone way too far!" My mom sounded shocked. She arranged for me to see a specialist in eating disorders, and I started getting help. It wasn't only about learning to eat healthy again. It was about figuring out why I'd gotten hooked on dieting in the first place. About how I thought being thin was going

to be the answer to all of my problems. About figuring out other ways to deal with my feelings besides this crazy dieting, and about getting back the life and the friends I'd been ignoring.

Jeannie, 15

If Jeannie's story sounds like it could be about you or someone you know, you can get help, too. See the back of this book for suggestions. Remember, it's best to catch this behavior early, before you get really stuck.

Drinking and Drugs

Every teenager knows that you're not supposed to drink or do drugs. But plenty do it anyway. Some do it to be cool. Some do it to escape from their problems. Of course, the truth is that drugs and alcohol add more problems to your life.

When I first started going to these coed parties in eighth grade, I was really nervous. I thought I wasn't any fun and no one would like me. It was getting me down. This friend suggested I drink something to loosen up. It tasted awful but worked for a while—then I had to keep drinking more to keep the feeling going. Then someone said cocaine would work quicker than drinking. It did, but the crash from coming off it was super quick and intense. I hated that feeling so much that I kept doing more and more coke just to avoid coming down.

Then one night I blacked out. When my older sister found out, she made me go to an AA meeting. First I was mad. I thought the meetings would be filled with old drunks, but it turned out they had teen meetings. It was weird, but I had to deal, and in the end that was a relief.

Courtney, 14

If you see yourself in Courtney's story, think about contacting AA (or another organization) for help. AA meetings work for both drug and alcohol addictions. The meetings are free and you don't have to sign up in advance. Just look up the listing for Alcoholics Anonymous in your local phone book, and call for meeting times and places. You don't have to give your name. The meetings are confidential. Besides, everyone there has a problem just like yours!

School Problems

I was like, who cares about school? So what if my grades go down? What's the big deal about being late for class? But they made me go to the guidance counselor. All my teachers said I had a problem. Me, a problem?

But, yeah, I kind of did. When I talked to Mrs. Ramirez, I ended up telling her about how my friends acted like they didn't know me anymore. And at home, no one was ever around. Working, working all the time. It was like everyone checked out. And Mrs. Ramirez, she said, "So, you checked out on school." It was like, okay, yeah, you got a point.

T.J., 13

Kids have trouble at school for lots of reasons. Sometimes it's motivation. Sometimes it's study habits. But sometimes it's depression. If you are feeling depressed, it is hard to concentrate and to put much effort into your work. It may be a struggle for you to go to school at all. Often school is the first place a depressed mood will show. Here are some signs.

Have you suddenly gone from a B student to barely passing?

Are you suddenly having trouble paying attention in class or finishing your work?

Are you giving your teachers a hard time in class?

Are you getting into fights with your classmates?

Have you basically stopped caring about how you are doing in school?

Are you finding every excuse in the book not to go to school?

Are you actually cutting school on a regular basis?

If you answered yes to any of these questions, your mood

may be messing you up at school. Try to figure out what the problem is. If it's gone too far for you to get a grip on yourself, see if your school counselor has some ideas about what will help you. That's what T.J. did.

Reckless Behavior

I don't know what came over me. I was shopping in Kmart and all of a sudden I had like this desire or like this need to slip this bottle of blue nail polish into my pocket without paying. I knew it was wrong, and I even had the money in my wallet. But I took it anyway. Store security stopped me and I was so scared I started to cry. They called my parents to come and get me. I've never seen them so mad! I'd never done anything like that before, and I couldn't even explain why I did it.

Cheryl, 13

Why did Cheryl do it? Her boyfriend had broken up with her two days before. She was feeling sad and rejected. Cheryl didn't realize it at the time, but somehow taking that nail polish felt like a way to get rid of those bad feelings. Of course, it didn't work—not for more than a second.

Cheryl was lucky she got stopped right there. Replacing feelings with actions can cause all kinds of problems—physical, emotional, and even legal.

Shoplifting is one kind of reckless behavior. So is running away, or driving drunk.

Sometimes kids use sex to try to get rid of their lonely, empty feelings. When people are feeling depressed, they can get mixed up about how to get what they need in life.

I just wanted so much for someone to love me. I thought if I had sex with whoever asked, then I'd never be alone. Then I saw this show on sexually transmitted diseases, and I got scared. I mean really scared. I went to Planned Parenthood and got tested. Now that I know I'm okay, I don't want to keep taking chances. They told me I have to get some counseling to stop mixing up sex and love.

Andrea, 15

Do you take risks like Andrea and Cheryl? If you have trouble controlling your behavior, it doesn't mean you're a bad person. Chances are there are serious problems in your life that cause you to act out. There's lots of help available. Just turn to the back of this book.

Slow It Down!

The kinds of depression that don't look like depression happen when people are looking for instant relief from bad feelings. But problems just multiply if you choose something addictive or unhealthy as your solution.

What else can you do? Try this strategy. When you notice that you're about to do something reckless, stop. Sit down a minute and think. Ask yourself, "What am I feeling and what

4

What You Can Do About It

Everybody knows that if you want to do well on a world history test, you have to study. Everybody knows that if you want to make the tennis team, you'd better practice. But a lot of people think that you can't do anything about your moods—that you're stuck with whatever bad feelings come over you.

That's not true. Of course, there are no magic spells that make bad moods vanish, but you can learn ways to deal with your feelings so that bad moods won't feel as bad or hang on as long. If you get depressed sometimes, learning ways to cope can help you keep minor depressions from getting worse. Then it will be easier for you to keep your life on track.

People look at me like, "this girl has got it together." They see my grades, my boyfriend, my activities. They don't have a clue what it took for me to get there. When my parents split up, my life got really confusing.

One weekend here, one weekend there; everything I took for granted had changed. I spent a lot of time just feeling rotten. But after a few months I realized that unless I figured out how to keep my life going in the right direction, I would end up all messed up. It took a lot of work, but it was definitely worth it.

Sarah, 17

Health Watch

The very first step to feeling good emotionally is making sure that you are okay physically. Sometimes depression is actually caused by physical illness. Certain medications can also affect mood. A checkup with your doctor will let you know that everything is fine—or what to do if it isn't.

Then there's *staying* healthy. People have probably been lecturing you forever about things like getting enough sleep and eating right. But how much sank in? And did it really make sense to you? Take this quiz to see how much you know about being smart about your health!

HEALTH QUIZ: True or False

1. Everyone's weight goes up and down by a few pounds each month.
2. If you're thin, it's fine to eat tons of sweets.
3. Some people need more sleep than others.
4. You should avoid snacking.
5. There is no such thing as a caffeine buzz.

6. Drinking water is important only if you sweat a lot.

7. Only little kids need milk.

8. Keeping your weight down is the main reason for exercising.

ANSWERS

1. True. Small weight changes are entirely normal and natural.

2. False. You'll find you feel better if your diet is healthy and balanced, rather than high in sugar. In fact, some nutritionists say that too much sugar can make you feel anxious.

3. True. Try to figure out how much sleep is right for you. Sleeping too little can make you irritable and interfere with your ability to concentrate. But be careful about sleeping too much. That can make you feel even more tired.

4. False. Healthy snacks, like fruit or yogurt or crackers, are fine. In fact, it's a good idea to have one sometime between lunch and dinner to keep your energy (and mood) up.

5. False. Caffeine is a powerful drug. It can make you feel wound up, irritable, and anxious.

6. False. Drinking water—a lot of it—is good for you in many ways.

7. False. Everyone needs calcium, which milk supplies. If you don't drink milk, get calcium in another way—through other dairy products or calcium substitutes.

8. False. Exercise keeps you fit, gives you energy, strengthens your heart, and even helps your state of mind.

So, how did you do?

Of course, knowing what's healthy and actually living healthy are two different things. Just remember, your feelings are definitely affected by your physical health. So be careful about the kinds of food you eat and the amounts of sleep and exercise you get.

Taking Care of Your Feelings

What can you do with your bad feelings? Sometimes it seems as if no one wants to know about them. You don't end up with a lot of friends if you are always pouting about something. Aren't the people who are always cheery the popular ones?

Everyone knows that "I'm fine" is the answer you are supposed to give when someone asks, "How are you?" But what happens when you really are not fine?

People need a way to express how they feel about what is going on in their lives. No feeling is as bad as one that stays locked away inside.

Express Yourself

How do you cope with feelings? Everybody's different. See if you can find what works for you. Here are some ideas.

Sometimes my friend Katrina and I get a huge piece of paper, and we write down everything and everybody that pisses us off. When we're done, we tear it up into little tiny pieces. You'll probably think that's wacked, but we think it's fun!

Melissa, 15

My friends and I have a sleepover. By the time midnight comes, we have talked about everything.

Jenna, 13

I get on my Rollerblades and go. After a few miles, all the stuff that was bothering me is just like easier.

Andrew, 14

I play bass. It's the best. All my emotions go into the strings.

Sam, 15

Okay, you'll think this one is weird, but if I am feeling so pissed off I can't stand it, I go into my room and punch my pillow. Hard!

Erin, 14

Easy. I draw. I have a huge drawing pad, and I get

out my pastels and use whatever colors match my mood. And, like, don't bother me till I'm done.

Michael, 16

I work on my comic strip. I started it last year when we had the worst substitute. Everybody thought it was funny, and I just kept on going.

Justin, 15

I put on my favorite CD and dance in front of the mirror. The music sets me free, and hey, the exercise doesn't hurt.

Tiffany, 14

I write in my journal. I've been keeping one since I was twelve years old.

Sarah, 17

Make Friends with Your Journal

A journal is a great way to express yourself. It gives you a private place to say whatever you feel like saying. The journal doesn't have to be fancy or expensive. It just needs room for your feelings. You can also write your journal on a computer, if you prefer. Here are some different ways to use your journal.

FREE WRITE

Start at the top of the page and write down whatever pops into your mind. Keep writing until you have filled the whole page. It doesn't matter what you write. Your handwriting and your grammar don't matter. All that matters is that you keep writing and don't stop until you get to the end of the page. Don't cheat and buy a tiny journal. Don't censor yourself, either. Free writing is a way to write yourself free. It's a chance to admit to yourself all of your feelings and thoughts—big, small, petty, silly, sad, mad, ecstatic, just fine, or way out there. Whatever they are, they are yours, and it helps to acknowledge them.

DRAWING

Drawing is another way to free yourself up. You don't have to be an artist to do it. Take a pencil and let it go. Doodle, scribble, fill the page with whatever design comes to you. Now try another page. Go ahead and draw a picture of something. It can be anything at all. Try colored pencils or pastels to express yourself through color. If your journal is on your computer, you can draw or paint there.

SECRETS

Do you have something that is bothering you? Like, say, secrets that you can't tell anybody? Something that happened that's too awful to say? Feelings you think are too dumb to waste paper on? Ideas that nobody would ever take seriously?

Take a section of your journal, or make up a special journal just for them. Your secrets and hidden feelings will feel less strange and embarrassing if you begin to write them down. Giving them a place will also help you feel less closed up inside.

You can also make a place for your dreams and secret wishes. Go ahead and illustrate it, if you feel like it. Let yourself know what makes you happy.

THE UNMAILED LETTER

Do you have something you'd like to say to someone, but you are afraid that speaking out would just make more problems? Or is the person not around to hear it? Here is a journal technique that can help you say it anyway.

Write a letter to that person in your journal. Don't worry if they won't like it; they are never going to read it. You can say exactly what you think and exactly what you feel! Now put the journal away, and know that you said it.

How's Your Mental Attitude?

Many people fail because they believe they will fail. Many people don't try because they think they can't do it. Many people don't make friends because they have decided that nobody likes them.

The opposite is true, too. Sports teams with a positive "mental attitude" are more likely to win. Optimism has amazing benefits. It even helps your immune system battle disease. Pessimism makes you more likely to get physically sick, and more vulnerable to depression.

What is your mental attitude? That's *not* the same thing

as the "attitude problem" that adults lecture about. They are talking about having respect. "Mental attitude" means your outlook on life.

TEST YOUR MENTAL ATTITUDE

Your family moves to Baltimore, right in the middle of the school year. Nobody seems friendly in your new school. Some of the kids look at you funny. They hang out in cliques, and you don't fit in. You think:

a) Nobody likes me in this school; there is no point in trying to make friends.

b) The way these kids look at me, I must be a loser.

c) If I cut class, I won't have to deal with this.

d) I'm new here, that's why they're checking me out.

e) There have to be kids here I can be friends with; I just have to keep trying.

You try out for the school play, but you get picked to be a stagehand. Your next-door neighbor gets the lead you wanted. You think:

a) I shouldn't have tried out. I just wasted my energy.

b) I guess I have no talent.

c) I hate her/him! Next time she/he wants something, I'll make sure she/he doesn't get it.

d) Maybe another time I'll do better.

e) I wish I had gotten the part, but at least I'll be part of the show.

Your parents have been fighting about where to go on vacation. You can hear them arguing through the wall, and it makes you nervous. You think:
a) I hate it when they argue; we just shouldn't go on vacation.
b) Okay, what did I do this time?
c) I'm running away.
d) I hate it when they argue, but I know it's their problem, not mine.
e) People don't always agree; I guess that even means parents.

You finally get your nerve up and ask that cute girl/guy to see a movie with you. She/he says, "I can't; I'm busy." You think:
a) That was a waste! I won't ask anybody again.
b) She/he hates me. I should have known.
c) I'm going to tell everybody that she/he's a dork.
d) Maybe she/he isn't interested, but I guess someone else will be.
e) Maybe she/he is really busy. We do have exams next week. I'll give it one more try.

You get a C on the biology midterm. You think:

a) That's it! My life is over!

b) I always knew I sucked at science.

c) Wait till Mr. Roper sits down on his chair tomorrow!

d) Not my best grade, but at least I aced the English exam.

e) I wish I had studied more; I better spend more time on biology next term.

SCORING

Count up how many times you chose each letter (how many A's, B's, etc.)

Which letter did you pick most often? _____

What letter came in second? _____

Did your answers fall mostly on one letter, or are they divided among two or more letters? Read about all the answers that apply to you.

Mostly A's. You have a tendency to give up in response to stress. When you feel like "I give up" or "It's hopeless," stop that thought in midair. Is there some way you can keep trying? Call a friend, or reach out to other people for some *en*couragement when you feel *dis*couraged.

Mostly B's. You have a tendency to blame yourself when things go wrong. When you think "It's all my fault!" challenge yourself. Is it really your fault? Is there another *realistic* reason for what happened? Sometimes you also jump to negative conclusions about yourself after one disappointment. Challenge that thinking, too. Are you being fair? Or did you let that thing that went wrong turn into the whole world? Try to get real with yourself. It will actually feel better!

Mostly C's. You tend to blame other people when things go wrong. If you are fuming about what someone did to you, take a deep breath. And another. Now, think, is it *all* his fault? Is there something besides who's at fault that's important to focus on? You also sometimes jump into doing things that you might regret later. Take a deep breath before you take action. Let your mind clear. Figure out what's really bothering you. Think about how you can handle the situation. What can you do that you won't regret later? What will make you feel responsible, and good about yourself?

Mostly D's, E's. You are able to take a realistic view of difficult situations. Keep it up!

Build Your Self-Esteem

Julianna felt lost when she started at her huge middle school, so she decided she just had to fit in with one group of popular girls.

Every time those girls walked by, they'd look right through me like I wasn't there. Then they'd go off whispering, probably saying how bad I looked. So I took my baby-sitting money and bought expensive new jeans, ones like Ashley's. But when I walked by, they kind of nudged each other, then looked through me worse than ever. I totally wanted to disappear.

At Thanksgiving, my cousin Marina came over. She wanted to hear all about school. When she found out what was going down, Marina said, "Girl, you are better than that! Tomorrow you go in there in your rattiest clothes. You walk right by those girls like 'I don't care!'"

All of a sudden I got what Marina was saying. So I did it. I put on the jeans I wore to paint my poster, and I walked right past where they hang out. When they started whispering, I stared right at them. I felt like, hey, if you don't like how I look, that is your problem. After that I made some friends who liked me the way I was.

Julianna, 12

When the popular girls treated Julianna as if she didn't exist, she fell right into the trap of feeling like there was something wrong with her. Her cousin reminded her of something else—her own value. Once Julianna remembered that, she could wear anything and look anyone in the eye; it didn't matter if they stared. She had her self-esteem back.

Self-esteem may be invisible, but it helps you more than the coolest clothes. Self-esteem is an inner feeling that you matter, no matter what. No matter how other kids treat you, no matter if your parents are mad at you, no matter what your grades are, or what goes wrong for you. Strong self-esteem helps you get through the stresses of life.

The opposite is true, too. If you feel shaky inside, it's all too easy to be crushed when things don't go your way. That makes you vulnerable to getting depressed.

Teenagers get their self-esteem challenged all the time. Friends can stop acting like friends. Other kids can put you down for not being the same as them. It is easy to lose track of who you really are if you are getting pressured to follow the crowd.

Jeff had always been about a head shorter than the other boys. It was no big deal; they liked him anyway. But when he moved to a new school in the seventh grade, the boys there started calling him "Jeffie" and shoving him when they passed by. In gym class, they snickered when he couldn't do a jump shot.

These guys treated me like a dork. It was no fair. So what if I'm short? But it started to get to me any-way. I'd walk down the hall fast so they wouldn't notice me, and I started to feel like maybe I was a dork.

Then at Christmas, I got a card in the mail from my old karate teacher, from where I used to live. That started my brain thinking, you don't have to take this lying down! I found a new sensei and went at it till I passed every level.

"This man's a Black Belt!" My gym teacher let everybody in class know I made it. So they started treating me like one of the guys, and that was definitely better. But the best thing was I had my old self back, and nobody, not nobody, is messing with that again!

Jeff, 13

Don't let someone else define you. It is up to you to decide who you are and who you want to be. Don't let anyone take that away from you.

How is your self-esteem? Do you feel like you are not really important? If somebody ignores you, do you feel like you aren't worth paying attention to? If you answered yes to these questions, your self-esteem needs some positive attention.

Do You Have to Be Perfect?

Arielle got five A's and one B. That B spoiled her report card and her perfect 4.0 average. She felt terrible.

"So what? You still did really, really well." Her friend Meredith tried to make her feel better, but it didn't work.

Arielle started biting her fingernails again, even though she was trying to let them grow. It didn't help that she got one problem completely wrong on the next math test. "I'm so stupid!" she moaned.

There is nothing wrong with taking schoolwork seriously. It is serious. But if you believe that only perfect grades are

Self-Esteem Secrets

1. Get Off the Seesaw

Remember the seesaws in the playground when you were little? When one person is up, the other person is down. Lots of people play that  game without a real seesaw when they get older. In order to feel like they are better, they treat other people like they are worse. If that happens to you, get off the seesaw. Make a joke, walk away, talk to someone else. Show them (and yourself) that you don't find the game interesting.

2. Imagine

Do you have a situation that's bothering you? Close your eyes and visualize. How would you like to handle things? See yourself doing just what you think is right. Memorize that picture. It'll help your confidence next time you have to deal with whoever's giving you trouble.

acceptable, you are in trouble. The same goes for the perfect weight or the perfect group of friends.

Sometimes perfectionism comes from growing up in a family whose high standards leave no room for mistakes. Sometimes kids set their own very high standards. They decide that only perfect is good enough.

3. Role-Play

Try this with a friend. One of you can take the role of *the problem*, maybe the class bully or the teacher you hate. The other one can be you. Say what you wish you could say to *the problem*, then switch sides. You don't need to actually say these things in real life to whoever's giving you trouble. Just acting it out will help.

4. Get Strong

If you are feeling threatened or insecure, getting physically stronger can help your confidence. Take up a sport or some form of exercise. Or take a self-defense class. That way you will know you can take care of yourself. You don't ever have to use it; just having the knowledge gives you an edge.

5. Get Smart

Focus on something that really interests you—maybe a subject at school or a special hobby. Set some goals and go after them. Getting good at something is a sure way to build confidence.

High standards can help you succeed; they give you something to shoot for. But when perfection is the only thing that counts, it's a setup for disappointment. So remember, human beings aren't perfect. You'll be happier and no less successful if you give yourself a break.

Balancing Act

Do you expect yourself to be perfect? Are you setting unrealistic goals? Are you trying to do too much? If you are, then try this exercise to help get your life in balance.

1. Write down a list of everything you're involved with. Be sure to include things you have to do (no choice)—like school, or maybe baby-sitting your little brother, other household chores, religious school, et cetera.

    Label each activity A, B, C, or D. A is for most important; D is for least important. You're setting priorities.

    Now, think about your list. If you're feeling stressed, can you cross any of the activities off? First look at those labeled D. Any luck? Remember, you can also cut down on activities or stop some things temporarily during a high-stress time (like before exams!). You can take them up again later.

2. Now, try doing your schedule. Fill in each day of the week.

	A.M	P.M.	evening
Sunday			
Monday			
Tuesday			
Wednesday			
Thursday			
Friday			
Saturday			

Are you booked every afternoon? Every evening? Do you have time to do homework? Time to be with your friends? Time to be alone? Time to relax?

If you answered yes to the first two questions or no to any of the others, go back to your list and see what you can cut out. Or, if you don't want to drop anything, is there a way to change how much time it takes you? Keep prioritizing. These are skills you can use throughout your life!

I was on the girls' tennis team and practiced three days a week. Then I had this job at the video store and I was working twenty hours a week. I wouldn't cut back because I needed the same job full-time over the summer. I thought my boss might get mad at me if I asked to work less. The only time I could hang out with my friends was after my late-night shifts on Friday and Saturday around 11P.M., and I wasn't going to give up seeing my friends. Finally I got sick and had to stop everything for a while. The doctor said I let myself get really run-down. It was not a fun lesson. I won't stress myself out like that again.

Francesca, 16

There is no such thing as a life without stresses or obligations. The trick is to figure out what's important to you. When you put your efforts into the parts of your life that really matter, then all that work isn't just a pain; it's something you feel proud of.

All Stressed Out?

Who hasn't been? With all the pressures on teens today, getting stressed happens.

Stress makes you tense and speeded up. Too much stress

can make you more likely to get sick, depressed, or to just plain crash. But what can you do about that?

It's not your fault when stress happens. It's not your fault if your science teacher and your English teacher both decide that Friday is a great day to have a test, and your parents decide that Thursday night is a great night to have your relatives over to tell you all about their trip to Yellowstone, and your friends call on three-way because they *have* to tell you what they heard this guy saying about you, and…it is *not* your fault!

So, what can you do about it? You can't stop everyone else from doing what they're doing, but you can help yourself relax.

Cool Down

Find a quiet place. Now, sit down and close your eyes. Breathe in and out slowly, evenly, in and out. Now, make your hands into fists. Ball them up as tight as you can, and then let go. Squish up your feet. Let go. Now your legs. Let go. Then your butt. Let go. Now, push your shoulders up to your ears, take a deep breath, and let them down again. Now, clench your jaw, and then relax it with a sigh or a hum or a breath.

Okay, now breathe deeply again, in and out, in and out. Think of a place that is peaceful, somewhere that makes you feel really calm.

Imagine that place. Notice the colors, the smells, the scenery. See yourself there in your mind's eye. Let yourself feel the calm of your special place.

Stay there for a while. When you feel good and relaxed, open your eyes. Now you can go back to your life. But hold on to that special place you found. You can visualize it whenever you need to relax.

Enjoy Yourself!

Look for easy ways to bring calm, peace, and pleasure into your life. Just like everybody has their own triggers for what gets them upset, everybody has their own triggers for feeling good, too. When you've been upset about things, or especially if you have been depressed, you can actually forget what brings happiness into your life! Here are some ideas.

- *Watch my favorite movie for the fifth or sixth time.*

- *Pet my cat. When she purrs it makes me happy.*

- *Get out my bike and ride.*

- *Listen to my favorite CDs while I sit on my bed with my eyes closed.*

- *Go to the library. Find a quiet corner. Read a good book where no one will bother me.*

- *Go skiing, skating, Rollerblading, waterskiing, anything like that!*

- *Bake cookies.*

- *Look through magazines and check out the fashions*

- *Go for a hike. Where I live, the mountains are unbelievable. As soon as I smell that air, I get a good feeling.*

How Other People Can Help

Talking with Friends

There's nothing like a good friend when you're feeling down, but that doesn't mean it's so easy to let them in on things.

I feel weird, talking about my feelings.

Everybody is so busy, I hate to bother them with problems.

Are those just excuses for not talking to anyone? Not really. Lots of times your friends *are* busy. And it can be hard to talk about important feelings, especially if you don't have much practice. But don't let that stop you from reaching out. Letting your friends know what is going on in your life can be a big relief. It can make you feel closer to them and less alone with whatever you are facing.

Remember Kim from Chapter 1? That's exactly what happened to her. Kim's friend Lena finally tracked her down and talked to her. Lena stopped Kim from feeling stuck with all the stuff that worried her. Just hearing her best friend's voice kept Kim from sliding down into a worse mood. And when Lena gave her some ideas on how to deal with school, Kim got her life back together.

That's what friends can do for you. But it doesn't always happen. It depends on what kinds of friends you have and how serious the problems are. Some problems are too deep for even the very best of friends to fix. That means you need to look farther, and get help from other people. But even then, it's still good to have your friends around, in the loop. Friends are for every kind of time you go through.

Talking to Parents

For most teenagers, talking to parents about personal problems is hard. How will they react? Will they respect what you have to say? If you are feeling depressed, talking to your mom and dad can be even harder. Here is what lots of kids worry about.

They won't listen.

They won't care.

They won't understand.

They are too busy to pay attention to me.

It will upset them too much.

They have too many problems of their own; I don't want to make it worse.

They will overreact and go crazy on me.

They'll get all overprotective.

They'll get mad and say I let them down.

I don't even think they'd be so bad; I just don't like them knowing my business.

Okay, now we have ten reasons *not* to tell them what's wrong. But here is a big reason to do it anyway—they are your parents. Even if hearing about a problem does upset them, they would probably rather know. Just about all parents care about their kids a whole lot. If you give them a chance, they just might surprise you and understand.

I never talk to my parents. I mean, when I was six years old I used to come home from school and say "blahbety, blah, blah," but I haven't done that in a long time. But when everyone got asked to Ron's graduation party except me, I felt too embarrassed to say anything to my friends and I had to talk to somebody. Finally I gave in and told my mom. You know what she did? She said, "Ron made a big mistake!" I didn't believe it was a mistake, but I liked hearing it. She told me that if he didn't wake up and realize his mistake, we could do something special that day, whatever I wanted. I didn't even say no.

Tiffany, 14

But just like every teenager is different, parents are different, too. Some parents are much easier to talk to than others. Sometimes there are so many problems in your family that it's really hard to communicate. Sometimes you can't get your parents to take your problems seriously, even if you do try. If that happens, it's not your fault. Try reaching out to someone else—friends, a relative you are close to, a good neighbor, or a teacher or counselor at school. Who do you feel comfortable talking to? That's a good place to start.

Talking to Someone at School

For some kids, school is the first place to look for an adult who can help. It might be a teacher that you trust, your guidance counselor, or your coach. If you don't know who to talk to, make an appointment with your guidance counselor. It's his or her job to help you when you are having trouble. Your counselor can help you right there with some problems, especially ones that are happening in school.

Your counselor can also be your resource person. Counselors can find you a tutor or any other help you might need. They know what's out there in your community. If you're sliding into something serious like depression, and you need professional help from outside the school, they can help you set that up, too. They can also bring your parents in and explain to them what's happening.

Getting Professional Help

What if you've tried to get over your problems yourself, but they're still getting you down? What if you've tried talking to the people you know, but you're still having lots of trouble? What if, after reading this book, you think maybe you are in a depression? Those are all good reasons to go one step farther—get some professional help.

Deciding to get professional help for your personal problems is kind of like deciding to go to the doctor if you are sick. Usually if you are feeling sick, you take a few days to see if you will start to get better on your own. But if your sickness doesn't go away after a time or it seems to be getting worse, you make an appointment to see the doctor.

The same thing goes for getting help with your mood or your feelings. But not everyone sees it that way. Some people worry—if I go see a shrink, does that mean there is really something wrong with me? Will my friends think I'm psycho?

These are common fears, but getting professional help doesn't mean any of that. It means you are making the intelligent choice to do something about what's bothering you.

I was so scared to talk to a total stranger. I was

sure it would be an old bald guy who would fall asleep when I was talking or tell me I really was crazy. Lucky I was wrong. My therapist turned out to be a lot more regular than that.

She didn't think I was wacked, and she even liked my sense of humor.

Gina, 14

Different Kinds of Help

Therapy

Therapy is talking about your problems with someone whose job it is to help you work them out. It gives you a place to deal with whatever has gone wrong, with a person who isn't going to judge you, punish you, or get their feelings hurt by what you say. The therapist's job is to help you sort out your feelings and get your life going right.

In therapy, you get relief by just talking. But therapy also can help you build your self-esteem, solve your current problems, and learn *coping skills*. That means finding ways to deal so that you know what to do the next time something bothers you.

Individual therapy is what Gina had. That's when you meet with a therapist by yourself and talk about everything and anything you want. He or she won't tell your parents or your school what you are talking about. He'll respect your privacy—unless there's something really dangerous going on. Even then, he'll let you know what he plans to do. Sometimes it's helpful to bring your parents in for a session or two. That's something you can discuss with your therapist.

It feels good to talk about whatever I want, without worrying about what my friends or my parents would think of it. I can hear myself better at her office because there's no other stuff going on. No TV. No little sister annoying me. It's all about me.

Gina, 14

Group therapy means meeting with other people who are going through similar problems. That's especially useful for someone who has problems with alcohol, drugs, or eating disorders, who is dealing with an illness in the family, or who is recovering from a trauma. Talking with kids who understand from their own experiences what you are going through is usually a huge relief.

My little brother had been sick like forever. He was born with cerebral palsy and all these other problems. My parents are always taking him to doctors and worrying about him. I feel bad for him, too. But sometimes I get mad at how much attention my parents give him, and then I get all guilty, like I'm this really bad person. I was really getting depressed over it.

The social worker at the hospital said I should try this group for kids whose brothers and sisters were always sick, like my brother. Man, those kids had the same problems as me! They would get angry, then feel guilty, too! It was so cool to talk to people who could relate to what was going on with me. We shared stuff and we talked about different ways to deal with it. It made me feel better to know I wasn't the only one.

Brad, 13

Turn to the back of this book for organizations that help people find groups concerned with their particular issues. Often these groups are free or low-cost.

Sometimes you're not the only one in your family who's having problems. *Family therapy* is when the whole family meets with a therapist to deal with stress you're all going through, to solve family conflicts, and to work out better ways to communicate with one another.

So what if I stay out till one in the morning? Like, what business is it of Robert's? Before my mom decided to marry Robert, I never had a curfew. It was just me and Mom and she trusted me. All of a sudden he comes along with all those other kids, three of them! And he brings over all these rules.

I told him straight out, "You are not my father. I don't have to listen to you!" The more he bugged me about his sweet little curfew, the later I came home. It was war! When he tried to ground me for staying out late, I showed him. The next night I just didn't come home at all!

But then my mom freaked. She said, "We can't live like this!" She made an appointment with a therapist named Sheila who works with families. When Sheila met with us, she had us each tell our story. When I heard my stepbrothers talk it was like, I didn't even know them before. I was too mad to take the time to see if I liked them. Then Sheila met with my mom and Robert, without any of the kids—my mom said they were learning to "co-parent." And then I had to meet with Robert—just me, him, and Sheila. First I hated the idea. But he didn't turn out to be as mean as I thought. I guess it's better than war.

Caitlin, 15

Medication

Doctors sometimes prescribe medicine to help people with clinical depression, eating disorders, and the kinds of depression that don't look like depression. Medication used along with talk therapy tends to work better than medication alone.

These medicines, which are called antidepressants, usually take two to four weeks to build up in your body and "kick in." They don't fix what's wrong in your life. But they can lift your mood and help with sleep, energy, and appetite problems that come with a serious depression. Most people go on medication for six months to a year. Many go off it after a year and never need it again.

I just couldn't deal. The phone rang—I wouldn't answer it. Homework—I couldn't even start. I even stopped putting on make-up in the morning. It was too much trouble. All I could do was sleep. And when I woke up in the morning I still felt groggy.

When I told my therapist how hard it was to get out of bed, she told me it was a good idea to try medication. At first I couldn't feel anything, but after a month the black cloud sort of lifted. Even my friends noticed I was in a better mood. Finally I could start taking care of myself like I used to. Like, you know, getting up in the morning, getting ready for school. It was a huge relief.

Caroline, 14

Medication isn't for everyone. For one thing, it can have side effects that bother some people more than others. It's your doctor's job to decide if it's right for you. But for many kids with depression, medication—along with therapy—can make the world a much brighter place.

Getting Started

If you think you could use some professional help, how do you get it to happen? Your parents, your guidance counselor, or your doctor can help you find someone to talk to. If you are having trouble getting your parents to understand, you can show them this book. Are there any sections that especially apply to what you're going through? You can ask them to read those parts. You'll also find phone numbers at the back of this book that you can call for information.

Sometimes a parent or school person is the one who suggests getting professional help. Remember Zack from Chapter 1? That's what happened to him. After his dad got mad about his grades, he called the school. They set up a meeting with the guidance counselor and Zack's teachers. The meeting was to figure out what to do for Zack.

Zack's Story, Continued

I put my head on the desk during homeroom. I didn't want to know about all these people sitting in Mr. Klein's office, talking about me. I figured they're all in there saying I turned into the worst student they've seen in a very long time.

Then my homeroom teacher said to go to the office to join them. I walked slow, real slow. It was just my parents and Mr. Klein when I got there. And no one looked furious.

"Son, we've decided we need to get you some help so you can get back to keeping up with your school-work." That was my dad talking, the same dad that was so mad the day before.

"Do you know what the problem is?" my mom asked me.

I didn't say anything.

"I bet he'll be able to answer you better after he's had some help," Mr. Klein answered for me.

So that's how I got started seeing Dan, my thera-

pist. Did I want to go? No. But I kind of had to. Nothing was working in my life, and it was better than having everyone on my case.

And Dan, he was kind of cool. He looked me in the eye. He listened to me. He didn't let me get away with answering, "I don't know" to every question. I liked the challenge. It was like he wanted to know who I really was.

After a couple of sessions, Dan told my parents I was in a depression. He said it was a "moderate" one—I guess that meant bad, but not as bad as they come. He told me (and them) that he'd like to give talk therapy a good try, but that if I didn't get a lot better in a few months, we would need to consider having me take medication.

That was like a challenge, too. Beat that deadline. Maybe my soccer spirit was starting to come back. But that wasn't the biggest thing. The biggest thing was something I used to be so embarrassed of, I would've walked through fire to avoid it. He made me face my feelings.

In the first few weeks we went over what went wrong in my life. You know, the test, the grades, playing bad at soccer, giving it up. But when we got to Brian leaving, he stopped and looked me in the eye. "You must really miss him." I looked down at my Nikes.

"Zack, I'm gonna let you in on a secret. Men feel stuff, too. They even cry."

I felt it coming and wiped it away. But that was the start. That was the start of admitting my feelings, and that was the start of this big relief I began to feel. I got braver about letting Dan know stuff. He didn't think I was a wimp for missing my dog so much. He even looked like it made him sad, too.

The funniest thing was, walking out of his office from talking about sad stuff, I felt happier. My energy started coming back. I saw this cute girl in homeroom, and I thought, "Why not?"

So then one day I felt like kicking a ball around, just for fun. I got out my soccer ball, and knocked it around in the backyard. But then I got to this shed that Casey always used to jump out from, and I stopped. Stopped and put the ball away and went back to bed.

I almost blew off Dan that week, but I didn't. He said he was glad I came. When I told him what happened, we went over my feelings all over again— missing Casey, missing Brian, feeling like nobody's there. But this time Dan asked, "What do you think you can do about that?"

Me, do something about it? I didn't know what he was talking about.

"Think about it," was all he said.

So I did. And that night I E-mailed Brian, like this:

"Yo Bri, any life out there? Anybody know how to play soccer like us?"

I got up early to check my E-mail. It had one message.

"Hey Dude, what's up? Good to see your name across my screen. Yeah, there is life out here. But nobody, not nobody, plays ball like we did."

That was the beginning. After that we E-mailed anytime, day or night, and—boing—there'd be a new message. When I told Dan about it, he put out his hand for "slap me five."

So I took it from there. "Get a life,"  *I told Dan, "that's what I'm going to do, get a life." He said, "Go for it!"*

I applied for a summer job at a day camp, coaching sports. And I started to study. Mr. Klein got me a tutor to help me catch up. I started to practice for the fall soccer team. And yeah, I asked that cute girl out. I was busy, but I didn't quit going to Dan. He was kind of like my coach, and it made it easier to get it together, knowing he was there.

Questions Everybody Asks About Therapy

1. *What's the difference between a psychologist and a psychiatrist?*

   A psychologist has a Ph.D., and a psychiatrist has an M.D. Both have advanced training, and both do therapy. Only psychiatrists prescribe medication, because psychiatrists have medical degrees.

2. *What about a social worker?*
   A social worker has an M.S.W. (masters in social work). Some social workers help people find the right resources for their needs, like say medical or housing problems. Many social workers do therapy, too.

3. *What if my family doesn't have money. Can I still get help?*
   YES. Most towns and cities have mental health clinics that offer what is called a *sliding scale*. That means that they can reduce their fees, based on your family's income. There are also low-cost referral agencies. Check the back of this book for resources.

4. *What about health insurance? Will that pay for therapy?*
   Many policies pay for some therapy. Ask your parents to check. They can get information by calling about "outpatient mental health coverage." If your family belongs to an HMO, they may offer the name of a therapist in their network.

5. *Will I have to go to the hospital?*
   Most depression can be cured by getting professional help in a therapist's office, not in a hospital.

But the hospital is there for dangerous situations. If you are suicidal or dangerous to yourself or others, the hospital is there to make sure you are safe. But most people stay only for a short time—from a few days to a few weeks.

6. *Will I have to have a physical exam, like I do at my regular doctor?*

   NO. Therapists do not do physical exams. They talk with you, and some therapists do activities like art, or even go for walks. But, it's a good idea to go to your regular doctor for a checkup, so the doctor can rule out any other type of illness that could be making you feel depressed.

7. *Do I have to tell my parents?*

   YES. Your parents need to know about going to therapy, just like they need to know about going to the doctor. They'll want to make sure you're in good hands. But they don't need to know everything you talk about. You have a say in that.

8. *What about other people? Will they talk behind my back if they find out?*

   No one else has to know unless you want to tell them. That's up to you. Lots of times a teacher you trust or a good friend is really glad to know. If you're worried about gossip, you can choose to tell only people you trust. But remember, no matter what anybody says, there's really nothing to be embarrassed about. Going into therapy happens to be a smart way to take care of yourself.

9. *What if I hate my therapist? Am I allowed to change?*

YES. Therapy works best if you *do* like the therapist. You need to feel that you can trust him or her. But before you change, talk it over with the therapist and with your parents. Sometimes people don't like their therapists because of misunderstandings. Sometimes it's because they didn't want to go into therapy in the first place, and they are not about to like *anybody*. But sometimes your therapist is just not the right person for you. Trust your intuition.

10. *How is therapy different from talking to a friend?*

When you talk to a friend, it can be embarrassing to admit certain problems. And sometimes a friend just doesn't know what you can do about them. A therapist knows about the kinds of problems people face. He or she has experience helping people find solutions.

11. *How long will it take?*

How long you go for therapy depends on how long you need to get over what's bothering you. Some people go for a few sessions, and some people go for a few years. There's no right or wrong about how long. The only thing that matters is getting there.

12. *How will I know if it's doing any good?*
YOU'LL KNOW. You'll know because you'll start to feel better. You'll know because you'll get more hopeful. You'll know because the problems that seemed impossible to get over won't seem impossible anymore.

Resources: Hotlines, Organizations, Websites, and More

Here you'll find addresses, phone numbers, websites, and special hotlines for organizations that are in the business of providing information to the public on depression and other problems. Most offer referrals—that means they can direct you to support groups, therapists, services, clinics, and/or programs in your area. If you call, remember the people who answer are there to help you out anyway they can. The hardest part is picking up the phone and dialing the number!

Low-Cost Therapy

Nearly every community offers a variety of low-cost therapy options. Your school counselor should be able to give you the names of local doctors and clinics that work on a "sliding scale," or, in other words, adjust their fees according to what a family can afford.

If your guidance counselor can't provide this information or you feel uncomfortable asking for help, go to your local phone directory. It should list community mental health clinics in your area in the business section of the white pages. Try looking up "counseling," or "mental health," or "family services." Clinics usually charge a lower fee than therapists who work privately. Many of the organizations listed below can also help with low-cost referrals. Just ask.

Hotlines

Hotlines are especially good to call in a crisis, or if you need immediate help or advice.

National Youth Crisis Hotline (24 hours)	800 442-HOPE
Covenant House Nineline (24 hours)	800 999-9999
National Boys Town Hotline (24 hours) This hotline is for girls, too.	800 448-3000
National Child Abuse Hotline (24 hours)	800 4-A-CHILD
National Domestic Violence Hotline (24 hours)	800 799-SAFE
Mental Health Hotline (24 hours)	212 734-5876
Suicide Prevention Hotline	212 673-3000
Narcotics Abuse Helpline	800 234-0420
Victim's Services Hotline	212 577-7777

Depression

These organizations are good sources for information about depression and for referrals.

Center for Mental Health Services
Knowledge Exchange Network
P.O. Box 42490
Washington DC 20015
800 789-2647
E-mail: ken@mentalhealth.org
www.mentalhealth.org

National Foundation for Depressive Illness
P.O. Box 2257
New York, NY 10016-2257
800 248-4344 (recorded announcement)
www.depression.org

National Mental Health Association
1021 Prince Street
Alexandria, VA 22314-2971
703 684-7722
800 969-6642
www.nmha.org/ccd

NATIONAL DEPRESSION SCREENING DAY
This is a yearly one-day event (usually held in October) offering adults and children free screenings for depression at thousands of places throughout the United States. Licensed mental health professionals

do all the screenings. Results are confidential. The NMHA is one of the sponsors. For more information, call 800 969-NMHA.

Depression and Related Affective Disorders
    Association (DRADA)
Johns Hopkins University School of Medicine
Meyer 3-191
600 North Wolfe Street
Baltimore, MD 21287
410 955-4647
202 955-5800 (Washington DC residents only)
E-mail: drada@welchlink.welch.jhu.edu

Special Resources

These organizations help people with specific concerns. Many of them run support groups and publish monthly news-letters. Ask for details when you call.

Attention Deficit Disorder

Children and Adults with Attention Deficit
    Disorder (Ch.A.D.D.)
499 Northwest 70th Avenue
Suite 101
Plantation, FL 33317
954 587-3700
800 233-4050
E-mail: majordomo@mv.mv.com
www.fmhi.usf.edu/chadd

Eating Disorders

National Association of Anorexia Nervosa and
    Associated Disorders (ANAD)
P.O. Box 7
Highland Park, IL 60035
847 831-3438
www.healthtouch.com

American Anorexia/Bulimia Association (AABA)
165 W. 46th Street #1108
New York, NY 10036
212 575-6200
http://members.aol.com/amanbu

Substance Abuse

National Council on Alcoholism and
    Drug Dependence (NCADD)
12 West 21st Street
New York, NY 10010
212 206-6770
800 622-2255

Alcoholics Anonymous
475 Riverside Drive
NY NY 10015
212 870-3400
www.alcoholics-anonymous.org

You can find listings in your area for AA and Alateen
in your local phone directory.

Learning Differences

Learning Disabilities Association of America
4156 Library Road
Pittsburgh, PA 15234
412 341-8077
w.ww.idanatl.org

International Dyslexia Assocation (IDA)
8600 La Salle Road
Chester Building
Baltimore, MD 21286-2044
301 296-0232
www.interdys.org

Children's Rights

Children's Rights of America
8735 Dunwoody Place
Suite 6
Atlanta, GA 30350
770 998-6698